The Pro[...]
Success Formula

*How we walked away with £150,000
using none of our own money.*

*Best of
luck in your
property journey
Chris + Mary*

CHRIS & MARY SELWOOD

The Property Success Formula

How we walked away with £150,000 using none of our own money.

Foreword

Isn't it a great thing to watch ordinary people accomplish extraordinary things?

There is nothing quite as exciting, (and nerve wracking…), as witnessing the trials and tribulations that one has resolved to endure, to reach new heights, achievements and success.

For any of us to accomplish such feats, we have to be willing to endure tremendous uncertainty and resistance and have a deep belief that no matter what, we will triumph in the end.

And in order to achieve anything truly worth having, we must be prepared to work harder and make greater sacrifices than most people would be willing to…not just for a day, a week or a month…but for years!

And this is exactly what Chris and Mary Selwood have done, and still continue to do, to this day!

I have watched them both dig deep to find ways to create new opportunities, to learn and implement new ideas and strategies for success. Not just in property, but in their personal growth and contribution to helping others. From the humble beginnings at Belfast

Property Meet, where their only ambition was to create a place where like-minded people could come together, to learn and share ideas with each other, and to help each other succeed in property.

They have also created their online monthly membership platform "Property Success University".

(www.propertysuccessuniversity.com).

So why don't Chris and Mary take all of that additional time, energy and resources and simply focus them on serving their own goals? Wouldn't it just be a lot easier to take everything they have learned from all the years of ups and downs, costly decisions, bad deals, sleepless nights and use it for their own benefit?

Of course it would, but then we wouldn't have the Chris and Mary Selwood's of the world who have a deep sense of responsibility to contribute to the success of many, rather than just the few.

Chris and Mary are two of the most extraordinary, resourceful and knowledgeable people that you will ever have the pleasure of knowing, who always go out of their way to help others succeed and avoid the costly mistakes they have made along the way.

I believe that one of the greatest things we can do in life is help the person who is struggling to find their way out the trenches…the one who just needs a hand up.

It's called contribution and it's what drives Chris and Mary to continue to host "Belfast Property Meet" and "Property Success University" as it's not about money, it about contribution.

Within the pages of this book that you are about to read, (and study), you will see contribution at work. You will come away with insights and knowledge that will compress decades into days. Most importantly, you will learn what can be accomplished where there is determination, creativity and belief in oneself.

BRIAN MULDOON

Contents

Chapter 1

We Got What We Focused On

> *Quote "If you always do what you've always did, you will always get what you've always got"*
>
> **Albert Einstein**

If you are reading this book, then you are most likely looking to make some changes in your life, to make things a little bit better than they are right now. If that's the case, then please read on because what you are about to discover could seriously change your life and that of your family.

If the reason is that you would like to make some changes, and that's the reason why you bought this book, then we would like to thank you. Our goal is to teach you the FORMULA that helped us to finally get out of the "Rat Race" and into a life of financial freedom. Our property success **FORMULA** has given us more choices and a much better lifestyle than we used to have. Our life is now much better than back in the days when we were in dead end jobs working for wages instead of profit. Now we're going to reveal how you can do this too. The FORMULA we came across has been so successful that we still use it to put together bigger and more profitable deals than we ever felt possible. The formula is not rocket science. You don't need to be a genius to use it. In fact, it's fairly easy to follow and with a few simple changes, and a few small steps, you can use it to build great wealth for you and your family.

The reason why we want to share this formula is that we know a lot about the kind of people who will buy this book and read it right through to the end. The kind of people who have a deep desire for a better lifestyle, more freedom and more choice. They want to have more control of their lives and the direction they are going. They want a better lifestyle, a nicer car, a nicer home, more holidays, new clothes, money to pay their kids' education or to pay the deposit for their children's first home. They also want the freedom to take those holidays whenever they want, not whenever they can get time off work! They also want to be able to choose the thing on the menu that they **REALLY** want, rather than settling for something they can afford, or to stay at the best holiday resorts not just the cheapest. You see, being thrifty with your money, constantly seeking out the cheapest thing in life takes as much energy as learning how to change your future. Unfortunately, 80% of us will choose to be thrifty and will constantly seek out a cheap lifestyle. The other 20% will seek the knowledge to change the direction of their life. Unfortunately 80% will do absolutely nothing with it. This 80/20 rule is called Pareto's Principle, the "law of the vital few" or the "principle of factor sparsity". Of the 20% who decide to take this knowledge and put it to good use, yes, you guessed it, only 20% will succeed. The other 80% will give up when the going gets tough, or when challenges appear, or they feel a little bit uncomfortable. Unfortunately thats what most people want. They want to be comfortable, however success is probably going to happen outside your comfort zone. So, where were we? Oh yes, were down to the 20% of the 20% which is just under 1% of those who started. 1 out of every 100 people.

Can you see yourself sticking with the thrifty lifestyle, stuck in your comfort zone or can you see yourself changing your life forever? Can you imagine yourself having a better lifestyle, more freedom and more choice to do the things you've always wanted but couldn't due to your financial position?

Once you have a clear mental image of where you want to be in the next 12 months, you have to make the decision that settling for an average life isn't going to get you fired up. In 2 years, 5 years or 20 years from now, will you have taken the right action to make it happen or not? Will your headstone say, "Here lies (Insert Your Name), died with potential fully intact."

What I'm about to point out might seem harsh, however, in order you to reach the pinnacle of the success that you truly deserve and desire, you have to be honest first and foremost with yourself. You have to make the decision that staying in your comfort zone is not going to cut it and that you will take the first step towards a better life.

If you put an action plan together will you commit to learning, to growing and to stepping out of your comfort zone or will you give up at the first sign of a problem? The late great Jim Rohn is quoted as saying "If you don't design your own life plan, chances are you'll fall into someone else's plan. And guess what they have planned for you? Not much! Why is it that most people fall into someone else's plan? Because we make excuses. We can make excuses, or we can make money, but we can't do both. The most common excuse is "I don't have time because I'm too busy". Unfortunately too many people are too busy watching soap operas or posting on social media. You are either making money or you aren't.

Most people are waiting for life to happen to them while others are out there making things happen. Once you've made the decision that you are going to take time to build a better life you must work hard, at the right things and work smart. When you put time and effort in, things start to flow and things start to happen. To become part of the 1% that we talked about earlier may seem a little far-fetched or out of your depth but bear in mind that 1% of the world's population is just over 75 million people. How hard can it be to get into the top 1%?

You've got to want to change. You've got to have some goals. You've got to have an action plan then fully commit to being successful. No shirking, no being lazy, no half-hearted attempts and no giving up, ever. The harder you try, the luckier you will get. One of the reasons why we wrote this book is too dispel the myth that successful people are just lucky. A study showed that self-made millionaires fell into 3 categories. Starting with nothing, the first group, THE SAVERS, took an average 32 years to become millionaires and ended up with an average of $3.4 million. They were more risk averse compared to the other 2 groups. The second group, THE EXECUTIVES, took 25 years by using company shares, big salaries and bonuses to average $5 million. The third group, THE ENTREPRENEURS, took just 12 years and ended up the wealthiest with an average of $7.4 million, through building businesses and investing in property and other investment classes. So you can see that the right type of hard work pays off and the " luck "will follow as a result. Unsuccessful people are likely to 'play safe' be totally risk averse, keep their money in the bank and they work hard for someone else will little or no ambition. They may also focus on delayed gratification i.e., building a pension and living a frugal life.

Successful people know that success leaves clues. They follow people who are successful and learn from them. They work hard on 'their plan' not other people's plans. They know success involves risk at times and that sometimes the greater the risk the greater the reward. They learn about and understand the risks involved, they set goals, write action plans and become fully committed to achieving success.

This book is designed to help your think beyond your limiting beliefs, the beliefs that stop 99% of the population from joining the other 1%. In 2017 we started an online training platform called Property Success University to help people achieve their property and wealth goals, faster and easier. For more information visit (www.propertysuccessuniversity.com)

We have coached many people over the years and what we have found is that almost all our coaching clients had the same fears we had before they started working with us. They were also frustrated with their job, because it took up so much of their time and was one of the biggest reasons they weren't living the life they desired. A full time job takes up about 1/3 of your adult life. The average 40-hour week plus commuting time takes roughly 1/3 of your time. When you think that most people sleep almost 1/3 of their day it only leaves one third to take care of everything else such as social activities, family time, washing, cleaning, shopping's, keeping fit, taking the kids to school or anything else you can think of. With such a huge chunk of your life spent working and travelling it's understandable that people get frustrated. It's even more frustrating if you're in a job you hate, working with people you don't like. The dream of giving up a job you don't like can bring about a strong and powerful motivation so it's easy to see why so many of us have this as our number one goal.

Another aim of this book is to help you make sense of the desire to quit your job and make a better life for yourself and your family. Our goal is to help you achieve a better lifestyle, more freedom and more choice. If this is what you want then our formula for success along with a plan and a commitment, will help you achieve that goal. If you are prepared to put in the time and energy to achieve your dreams, then please read on.

"If You Change the Way You
Look at Things, the Things You
look at Change"

WAYNE DYER

Chapter 2

If We Knew Then What We Know Now

> *"Formal Education will Make You a Living, Self Education will Make You a Fortune"*
>
> ***Jim Rohn***

WE BOTH GREW UP in working class families with the same values and beliefs as most people. We believed that hard work and hard work alone would bring you what you wanted in life. There's more to it than that. I was born in Ballymena in Northern Ireland, an industrial town with several big factories and quite low unemployment. Despite this fact, I went to live and work in Epsom, Surrey in England where I met Mary. Mary had trained as a nurse in both the learning disabilities and the general nursing fields. We went back to Ireland in 1996 to get married in Mary's home town in County Cavan in the Republic of Ireland. Shortly after we got married I began working in the Merchant Navy for various shipping companies. When our new born daughter arrived in 2003 it became a struggle with me being away at sea and Mary working full time as a nurse. From then on, despite fairly good salaries, the focus needed to be on getting a job at home and contributing to a pension. We started investing in property in 2005 primarily as a pension for me. Mary already had a superannuation pension through her nursing job in the National Health Service. We had heard about other people who were investing in the property market in Northern Ireland. We had no knowledge or practical experience of either buying or fixing up properties. The first property we bought needed fixed up so we had to learn on the job. We didn't have a pot of money to buy a property, but we realised that we could draw down on the equity on our own home for less increase in our monthly payments than we first thought. We invested about £13,000 in the deposit, survey, legal fees and refurbishment of a 2-bed mid terrace on the edge of the town centre of Ballymena. We had huge fears about what might go wrong as we embarked on this journey. We were scared of not being able to find a tenant. We had a fear of someone trashing the property and a fear of having to pay the mortgage out of our own pocket. Despite these fears there was still a sense of excitement. We could learn as we went along. We could also draw on our knowledge from seeing other people doing the same on BBC's Homes Under the Hammer. (Not a good idea). The one thing we realised about our fears and apprehensions that we didn't know back then was that we were totally focused on what could go wrong. We focused on potential problems and when you focus on something the odds of getting it, increase. What we should have done was focus on problem solving. Once we realised that focusing on the solution to a problem was better than focusing on the problem itself, things looked and felt a lot better. In Chapter Four we will dig down deeper into dealing with fears, confidence, problem solving and other things that come from within and that tend to get in your way all the time. When you learn how to overcome these mindset issues you will realise that tackling them is a vitally important part of building a property portfolio or a property business. So be prepared to change your mindset so that you can live the life you desire.

In Chapter Three not only will we share the exact formula we used to generate £150,000 but also how we raised several hundred thousand pounds for numerous projects over the last couple of years. We will also provide you with the templates and documents that we used as an added bonus.

Some other good news! If you are starting out as a new property investor and have no knowledge, skills or experience we will share a number of investment strategies that are working in real estate, right now. These same strategies can also help the more experienced investor take things to the next level. At this point we must we must remind you that property investing isn't a walk in the park. With some careful planning, taking the right action and with the right support, it can be exciting, inspiring, enjoyable and fulfilling.

We jumped straight in without knowledge or experience and made lots of mistakes early on. You don't have to make the same mistakes if you follow some basic principles for property investing success. If we knew then what we know now, we would have made a lot fewer mistakes. We would have lost less money buying the wrong properties and would have avoided trying to invest abroad until we had a bit more experience. In the early days we thought that we only had to buy a property and it would go up in price. It was this idea that caused us to buy properties at the wrong time, at the wrong price, in the wrong areas from the wrong people. Back then we paid sourcing fees for properties we could have bought on the open market without paying any fees whatsoever.

We weren't getting properties from sourcing agents at a discount. We bought properties at open market value and those fell in value in the property crash of 2008. Some of them ended up in negative equity but thankfully prices have recovered. We have also had time to pay down the mortgages in the last 10 years. Instead of buying regardless of price, paying full market value and not Below Market Value (**BMV**), we weren't concerned at that time because as we thought property prices would continue to rise, forever! We should have invested for cashflow only. We were lucky in a way that we did have a bit of cash flow from each property. If we had been cleverer we could have used the same funds that we had acquired to invest in cheaper properties therefore buying more and increasing cash flow. Let me give you an example. We bought a 3 bed two-bathroom mid terrace in county Durham for £97,000 because we 'liked it', It looked good inside, nicely decorated, integrated white goods in the kitchen and was a good property. The agent told us we could get £550 per month rent. At that stage we were oblivious to terms such as yield or return on cash invested (R.O.C.I) but we were in tune with terms such a "we like it". What we didn't know at the time was that once purchased we would struggle to get £550 per month. (A 6.8% Yield) In fact we ended up waiting a month or two before ending up with rent of £450 per month (A 5.6% Yield). I'm not quite sure what we were thinking at the time but if we looked closer we could have bought 2 x 2 bed terraced houses in other villages nearby for just under £50k each and rent of £390pcm each. For a similar outlay we could have bought two properties with combined rent of £780 per month (A 9.7% Yield). The lesson we learned was that we should invest for cash flow at all times, and that buying more expensive houses doesn't get you proportionally more rent. Our lesson was simple. Do not buy properties just because you like them. The property market is cyclical and will always go up and down. If you keep your mortgage loans on a decent loan to value ratio and you invest for cash flow then you have a very good chance of surviving any future crash. Oh, and did I mention, do not buy property just because you like it. Again, wish we knew then what we know now.

"An Investment in Knowledge
Pays the Best Interest"

BENJAMIN FRANKLIN

Chapter 3

It's All About People

> *"Networking is an Essential Part of Building Wealth"*
>
> **Armstrong Williams**

For the last number of years, we have spent much of our time working on relationships in order to build a portfolio. By the time of financial crisis or recession in 2008 we had bought 10 properties mainly by using the equity in our own home and thereafter using equity in other properties as they went up in price. Before the crash a typical buy to let deposit in the Uk was 15%. After the downturn, this rose to 25%. As a result, any of our buy to lets that were bought using 15% deposits were now considered highly leveraged. We struggled to get mortgages and to make matters worse, our credit status took a hit in 2009. It was sink or swim time.

We had also just spent £20k on getting a property education and it was by far and away the best decision we ever made. Was it great value for money? We certainly valued it because of what it cost but in terms of opening our eyes to other property investing strategies it was definitely a wise move. So, invest for cash flow and get yourself a property education. An investment in knowledge pays the best interest, said Benjamin Franklin, and we couldn't agree more. Our property investing journey didn't start in earnest until we got educated in different strategies, worked on our mindset and began to run things as a business.

As a result of not being able to get mortgages, firstly due to being highly leveraged and then due to a bad credit score, we began to focus on building relationships with other investors primarily ones with funds but no time or no skills. We had been running an ad in a local paper using the headline "We buy houses, any location, any condition, Call Mary on 07891012345". We found that using a woman's name tended to attract more calls. We received a call from someone who was trying to sell his mother in law and father in laws house in Belfast which was 30 miles away. I went to visit this 2-bed semi-detached property which was located in a leafy suburb of Belfast. The bonus was that the owners, who were elderly, were preparing to move in with their daughter and son in law and they didn't want an agent "for sale" sign outside, nor did they want all, sorts of potential purchasers and time wasters viewing the house on a regular basis. We thought the property had potential due to its corner site location and huge side and rear gardens. To us, it looked perfect for an extension and a replacement garage. We agreed a price of £120,000, but the key to the deal was that the owner's son in law agreed to let us apply for planning permission for an extension and a replacement garage, before we completed the deal. The owners were in no great rush to leave and we were very confident that planning would be granted quite quickly. We have sought the expertise of an architect who surveyed the surrounding area. Most of the other properties in the area had been extended at some point so it looked like we only had one problem. How were we going to purchase this property? We didn't have £120,000 nor did we have access to a mortgage finance to complete the deal. The property was mortgageable, so we had to come up with a plan. Having spent some time with other investors who were cash rich but time poor we knew that we could potentially bring someone else on board. We brought two people on board. All three parties agreed on a Joint Venture (JV) agreement where one of them would get the mortgage and pay the deposit and then he and the other investor would fund the work. Mary and I would oversee the work, get quotes from builders and basically project manage everything. We were now joint venturing with other investors who didn't have the skills, knowledge or time that we had. The key was that they had funds and wanted to put those funds to work. At that time the banks were offering 1-2% on savings which was pretty good in comparison to what followed in the next 6-7 years. It didn't occur to us at the time, but we had just struck a deal to use "Other People's Money" (O PM) This was the solution to our problem and it has remained our key ingredient in all our property deals since then. It's easy to say that OPM is the secret, but its only part of the formula. Finding other people with money is a lot easier than convincing them to invest in your deals. I'll come back to that. We bought the property for £120,000, spent £110,000 extending it into the side garden and into the rear garden and replaced the old run-down garage. We put the property on the market with one agent for around £300,000 but there wasn't much interest. We changed agents, lowered the price to £275,000 and got an asking price offer almost straight away. The profit in the end was just under £40,000 which was split three ways. The return on cash invested for the two investors was 18%. They both invested around £72,500 and got back £85,833 each. We invested some time, skills and knowledge and got back £13,333. Not an enormous sum of money but for the time we spent pulling everything together, it was a good return. The lessons that we learned were invaluable and worth way more than the share of the profit. We had completed our first JV deal using other people's money and barring one or two challenges it worked out well in the end. For the next couple of years, we repeated this same process, find a deal, find an investor and leverage their funds while they leveraged our skills and knowledge.

We had stumbled across something that worked for us and that could work for anyone whose circumstances were the same as ours. Whether it happened by good planning or by accident it didn't matter. When we started out we had no idea about joint ventures nor using other people's money. We would have sold the deal on for a sourcing fee to someone else, but we managed to get the project across the line at a profit. It just worked.

Our next deal using purely other people's money was a 5 bed, 2 reception room property in need of major refurbishment in Belfast. I had organised an "assisted sale" deal with the vendor. She didn't have the funds to carry out the work and was happy to give us "caretaker ownership" to carry out refurbishment and a charge on the property for the sum of money equal to the amount of money we would spend on refurbishment plus a bit extra to protect our share of future profit.

We agreed to pay the vendor £35,000 for this run down house but only after getting it up to a marketable condition. We estimated that the works needed around £25,000. Again, it was time to use other people's money while we used our skills and knowledge. Another JV agreement was drawn up and the work got underway. The work took about three months, having started in early September. It was completed by early December. On completion the JV partner was so impressed with the completed product (a fresh modern looking HMO - House in Multiple Occupation) We had extended the kitchen through into an old boiler house, re-wired all the electrics , added a fire alarm panel, installed new fire doors on all bedrooms and living areas, replaced the windows with high efficiency PVC double glazing and converted a small bedroom into a bathroom. The total cost amounted to around £30,000 which was £5000 over budget, however we had a plan to re-coup the money. After meeting the JV partner on completion of the works he was keen to keep the property. He offered to fund the £35,000 purchase from the owner. We set the wheels in motion to get the property valued. To our surprise other similar properties in the area in good condition were valuing at £90,000 - £100,000. During the purchase process, the owner allowed us to rent the property which allowed us to recoup some of the outlay. Once the purchase was complete, we would have to wait for 6 months before to mortgage the property and pay back all the costs to date.

A mortgage was applied for in June/July of the following year (6 months later) and the proposed value was very cheekily put down as £110,000. Our thoughts were that the surveyor could down value the property which would still work for us. We had spent £65,000 plus purchase and survey costs, so £67,000 in total. To our surprise the valuer agreed with our £110,000 so a 75% loan to value mortgage of £82,500 was available. This meant we had recouped all the outlays and had cash left over. This was split between us and the JV partner and we now jointly owned a property with cashflow of £350 per month each. This was a classic example of leveraging other people's money, putting money in, getting all that money back out and having the potential of good cash flow for us if we kept the house. A win-win for all concerned. This worked well and could be repeated over and over again, to the benefit of everyone involved. Our confidence was soaring, and we were constantly on the lookout for something bigger, perhaps a small block of apartments.

At the start of this chapter I referred to spending a lot of our time building relationships with the right people. Spending time with the right people pays off. Spending time with the wrong people doesn't work. If you spend a lot of time with people who can't pay it is likely that you will end up not being able to pay as well.

One of my favourite quotes on who we should associate with comes from Jim Rohn. He claims, "You are the average of the five people you spend the most time with".

Success leaves clues so learning from successful people is a must. Take a minute or two, to think about who you spend time with the most and whether they are helping or holding you back. The reason why you should associate with successful people, for me, is two-fold. Firstly, you learn the secrets that made them successful and this makes them a potential JV partner or a source of Angel Investment finance (AI). They are also likely to know more wealthy people, and this can lead to a growing network of potential funders.

Building a network of potential funders played a massive part in our next big deal. Mary had looked at a run-down block of apartments in a leafy street in the BT9 postcode area of Belfast. The properties on the street had once been the homes of judges, bank managers, barristers and other well-paid professionals. During the boom years several properties had been brought for big money only for the recession to kick in and those properties fell in value and would then be repossessed by the banks. They would then sit there as an eyesore for several years. Mary found six apartments, run-down, and unoccupied for 5-6 years. The mistake that the owner made was two-fold. Firstly, he had advertised them on the "commercial" section of a local property portal, and secondly, he hadn't put up a "for sale" sign outside. They were on the market for "offers in the region of £395,000 "which was a little over £66,000 per unit. There was one offer of £230,000 which was considered far too low by the owner. We did some due diligence on the property and the area, and thought we could potentially make some money. The initial plan was to use bridging finance to purchase and refurbish the property, however the lender we had initially approached had stopped lending in Northern Ireland. This was where our experience in dealing with investors would need to kick in. We were able to find another bridging company that would offer a loan, but only 60% of the purchase price. We had offered £280,000 but the vendor wanted us to pay £300,000 so we split the difference and agreed at £290,000. 60% of £290,000 gave us £174,000. However, with broker fees, arrangement fees and the lenders legal fees plus our legal fees we ended up getting around £160,000. We needed another £130,000 including stamp duty to secure the deal. Now, having spoken at our monthly property networking event, Belfast Property Meet, stood us in good stead.

I'm a firm believer that presenting from the front of the room helps put you in a great position to raise funds for good projects. I'll discuss those skills in more detail in the next chapter. We had put together an investment proposal. When we asked people for their opinion on the proposal, some of them ended up asking questions and then investing in the project. We had previous JV partners who could invest and others who couldn't because they had other things on the go. Some of them then introduced us to their friends or colleagues. Again, the networking principle was working and the good thing was that our network was being built by other people that we had previously worked with.

At this point we had a deal agreed and we were short by £140,000 and that's before we turned the key in the front door to start work. It would seem like a long road at times during this project, however it seemed like a mountain to climb just to get the keys. I secured another £30,000 from a previous JV partner but not for as long as I had anticipated. We pushed hard for more investment and managed to find another £120,000 which left us with some money to start work after we got the keys. More on how the project went in a later chapter but I wanted to focus on the skills you need to get this kind of project over the line. They include the following-

- ❏ **Writing an investment proposal.** Seems a huge undertaking but we've saved you a whole pile of time by doing one for you. We provide a template in the bonus section at the end of this book

- ❏ **Develop Presentation skills.** They say that public speaking is one of the top fears of most people. For most people fear of speaking in public is due to a fear of failure, a fear of looking inadequate or a fear of forgetting what to say. Master this and you will take things to a completely different level. We have lost count of the number of times we have spoken, individually or together, discussing a deal, after which people in the audience approach us and ask for a private one on one meeting, A lot of these people end up being investors in our projects. They become hands free, hassle free investors getting great returns on their money. The result of this is there is a world of potential investors out there, untapped just waiting for someone like you to show them how to get a better return on their money.

❐ This also applies to many other people who have some savings tucked away in their bank accounts earning little or no interest. We speak from experience here . We got £40,000 of investment finance from someone who was earning 3% gross on their savings account, they invested in one of our projects and got 15% return on their cash. This was from a brief conversation about how my day was going as I dealt with an investment. The same person has continued to invest in other projects. One quick conversation with the right message relayed in the right way, resulted in this £40k investment. Again, mastering good presentation or communication skills opens many doors.

❐ **Hard Work.** They say that there is no such thing as a get rich quick scheme and that's quite true. Normally if someone gets rich quick it's because someone else loses out. Think pyramid and Ponzi schemes. When you create win-win scenarios for all concerned then everyone is happy. This takes an abundance of hard work, but is definitely worth it in the end. As we stated in the earlier chapter you will need to commit to hard work. Good things rarely come to lazy people. In the following exercise we would like you to ask yourself some questions. Take some time to answer them thoroughly.

- What do I want to achieve in the next 12 months?

- Why do I want to achieve this?

- What impact will it have on my life?

Once you done this we want to take you 12 months into the future and ask you the following questions. Again, take some time to answer these questions as thoroughly as possible.

- ❏ What cashflow will I have? (The money left from rental income after all expenses have been paid)

- ❏ How much cash will I have access to, to buy, refurbish or grow your portfolio.

- ❏ What new relationships will I have built that will have helped me get close to, or to help me achieve my goals.

- ❏ How much extra time will I now have now that I have achieved my goals? (If I have replaced my income and given up my job what will I do with this extra time to multiply my wealth?

- ❏ How much time did I put into achieving these goals, on daily, weekly or monthly basis. For instance did I put in 20 hours per month for 12 months to achieve cash-flow of £2500 per month?. That would be £125 per hour for every hour invested.

If you are struggling to answer some of these questions, which is normal then ask yourself these questions.

- ❏ What am I reading?

- ❏ What am I listening to?

- ❏ Who am I associating with and what influence are they having on me?

- ❏ What am I watching?

I give some recommendations in later chapters

There is no such thing as an overnight success. What you put in, will determine what you get out. So, what is the one small thing that you can do today that will bring you even just a small step closer to achieving what you really want. Achieving your goals is about taking positive action in many small bite size steps.

> The Chinese Philosopher Laozi said, "A journey of a thousand miles begins with a single step."

In business terms this means that all projects, plans or goals no matter how big or how difficult or challenging have a starting point.

Chapter 4

How to Stop Getting in Your Own Way

> "If You Want to Conquer Fear,
> DON'T Sit at Home Thinking About
> it, Go Out and Get busy"
>
> **Dale Carnegie**

The single biggest thing that holds most people back from achieving anything is "themselves". We are conditioned from an early age to be careful, play it safe, don't take risks, stick to what you are good at. This play it safe mindset grows stronger as we get older to the point where it stops us from "giving it a go" in case we fail and look stupid in front of others. None more so than public speaking. Most people dread public speaking so much that more people fear public speaking than death. So, at a funeral most people would rather be in the coffin than having to stand at the pulpit and make a speech.

A small number of people find public speaking easy or at least easier because they overcome those irrational fears. In this chapter we look at overcoming fears and improving our confidence. We also look at dealing with problems without emotion, seeing things for what they are and not what our emotions trick us into thinking they are. We also cover how to focus on what you want instead of focusing on the things we don't want.

Let's start with **FEAR**. False Evidence Appearing Real. F.E.A.R. is a destroyer of many great things and the thing that takes away true freedom. The freedom to experience quality lifestyle. Most of us will avoid the life we truly want because of FEAR.

Our biggest fear is failure, the fear that you won't be good enough and that you'll look bad or stupid in front of others. Fear is nothing other than bad mind management, yet it paralyses us as if we are in real danger, such as physical harm or even death. Fear is OK when it makes us flee pain, danger or a struggle but it also holds us back.

Take a minute to think of one or two occasions when fear held you back, and I'm talking about a fear that seemed worse than it turned out. Going back to public speaking, let's think about the fear that we experience. Is it a fear of being physically attacked by the people you are talking to? Can you ever remember anyone speaking on stage and being attacked? Fear plays tricks on you mind by making you think that avoidance will keep you safe, but avoidance will stop you from growing and therefore stopping you from getting what you want. Most of the fears we harbour have nothing to do with physical harm, but they are fears of other things such as fear of rejection, isolation, failure and abandonment. These are emotional fears not physical ones.

The fear of public speaking is definitely a fear of emotional discomfort and not physical safety one.

- ❏ How will I look?

- ❏ Forgetting your lines

- ❏ Being judged by others

- ❏ Looking stupid in front of others

To overcome or control our fears we must recognise the effects they have on our lives. They almost force us to withdraw, they narrow our thinking, sap our energy and steal our courage. They restrict our personal freedom, play havoc with our confidence and can leave us powerless, feeling inferior and ready to quit when it fear shows up.

How many people do you know who are good at something yet never excel at what they are good at because of their fears. Fear stops them from changing, growing or innovating. Fear causes atrocities, marriage failures, hatred, lack of respect, lack of progress and insecurity.

If we let it, it will rule our lives. Fear can be activated or not. If you don't think that's true, then how do firefighters enter burning building or police enter a siege scenario or soldiers go into battle. The reason why those people can do those things is because they constantly choose bravery over fear otherwise fear wins. Choosing fear can sometimes be the easy way out because avoiding doing something difficult, courageous, challenging or scary is easier than doing it. It's hard to go to the gym 5 times a week. It's easy to sit at home and watch TV. It's easy to eat at fast food outlets but it's harder to shop for healthy food and cook yourself healthy meals. It's easy to drive everywhere. It's harder to walk everywhere. Fear, like many other things is socially conditioned. As toddlers we were inquisitive by nature, but we are moulded by our parents into being careful and playing it safe. This continues in adult life with our peers telling us to stick to what we're good at. We can now see that choosing fear over courage or fear over "giving it a go" is exactly that. A choice.

When you choose fear you are choosing not to overcome fear. Things that happened in the past should not necessarily influence future outcomes. You cannot control what happened in the past, but you can control how we react to the things that rise our fears today. We need to recognise the things and the people that brought us fear and anxiety in the past and try to avoid them. We mustn't allow other people's fears to get mixed into our decision-making process. Avoid the "worrier" and attract the "warrior". This will help you avoid those fears or at least help you deal with them.

Confidence - Working on your confidence is also a key ingredient for being successful. One of the best ways of building your confidence is to put maximum effort into your day. When you get to the end of each day and have given it your all, it works wonders for your confidence. When you've given your best you feel good about yourself and when you feel good about your self, your confidence starts to rise. The late, great Jim Rohn claims that self-confidence comes from the lack of neglect. If you neglect the simple daily disciplines. Self-confidence means doing whatever it takes. Don't just do it for a little while and see what happens and if that doesn't work, give up. Don't give up, keep going and then keep going even more but don't give up. If you need to change the people you hang out with then do it. If you need to change the books and magazines you read, the TV programmes you watch, the online content you view, the things you listen to, then do it. I remember when I first had the idea of starting a property networking event in Belfast in 2011. I knew about property investing but knew nothing about running or hosting an event and could not think of many things worse than talking in front of a group of people. When it was my turn to speak I couldn't look at the audience. I was as extremely nervous and was looking forward to sitting down. When I stood up to speak, my confidence sat back down again. I realised that I couldn't build a good network event if I wasn't prepared to grow as a speaker. It took me several years to get my confidence but only because I tried my best to avoid it. I didn't prepare well which in turn raised my fears and affected my confidence. Taking small steps such as practice, preparation and using notes or any other visuals aids would have improved my speaking ability much quicker. I avoided the small disciplines and hid behind my fears. I can assure you that once you learn public speaking it does wonders for your confidence. Whilst I still have a lot to learn about public speaking, I have spoken regularly at my own event and other events. Self-confidence also comes from rising above the negativity that surrounds you. Getting sucked into all this negativity damages your self-confidence and makes it easier for you to quit. This can generally puts you in a bad mood. How confident do you feel when your mood is bad? Having lack of self-confidence is like driving through your life with the hand brake on. Self-confidence is something we need to work on. When you see someone, who oozes self-confidence its most likely that he or she has been working on it for years. Self-confidence is something that is worked on and gets stronger over a period of time. We are constantly being bombarded by things that can affect our confidence whether its comments from your friends, family or work colleagues or its opinions that differ greatly from our own. Here are some of the things that you can do to improve your confidence.

- *Visualisation* - Visualise yourself as a very confident person-How does that feel?

- *Affirmation* - Practice affirmations and be grateful for all that is good about you and your life

- *Question the inner critic* - We are our own worst critic. Try approving of yourself instead of criticising

◻ *Adopt an equality mentality* - You are as good as the next person and you should stop wanting to be someone else. Be yourself and love yourself for what you are.

◻ *Focus on winning not losing* - Focus on your successes and forget about your failures. See the failures only as a learning curve and celebrate your successes. Go on, reward yourself, praise yourself and say it out loud.

Problems - Too often we become overcome by problems, challenges, obstacles, hurdles or whatever we want to call them. The reason why we get overwhelmed is due to the emotion or meaning we give to any particular issue. Why can one person deal with a problem in a calm relaxed manner yet someone else deals with it extremely differently. One is relaxed and calm and the other is an emotional mess. The emotional attachment we give to a problem defines how we manage it. Calling it a problem instead of a challenge can have a negative effect on how you see it. A potential problem or challenge may have many layers to it and when each layer is looked at individually it can make a problem seem like a series of minor issues.

Writing things down not only creates some clarity and focus but it can also act as a record for future challenges. When a challenge arises, we should look at how we would ideally like to solve it. What would be the ideal outcome and what is the likelihood of achieving that outcome. Would other outcomes solve the issues? Is there more than one answer? What will happen if the worst possible outcome occurs? What impact will that have on you or your business? When you decide what decision you are going to make then take full and complete responsibility regardless of the outcome. If you make the wrong decision and no one is hurt or injured, then its maybe not the end of the world. We're back to the fear of failure again. The fear of failing is nearly always a lot worse than failure itself. If you see failure as a learning curve then failing can have its positive impact on your personal growth. Once you've decided the solution to the problem and accepted responsibility, you should set a deadline. A decision without a deadline is meaningless discussion. You aren't off the hook just yet. When you've done all this then go and take action. Get busy, get urgent, get it done!

Focus - You can be fearless, have loads of self-confidence and be a great problem solver but lack of focus can definitely throw you off track. There are so many distractions these days from social media, pop up adds, emails, phone calls and whatever else the world is chucking at us these days. We are literally scared of missing something. I hear focused people say that if anything in the news or anything important is meant to reach you then someone will get in touch. We don't need to be constantly in touch with everyone for every minute of the day. I suggest you try a news blackout for 30 days to see if it makes a difference. The majority of news is negative and can have a huge impact on our mood, which then impacts our focus, which impacts our actions and productivity. Unfortunately, you may have to avoid social media as much of the negative news ends up being shared by your friends on platforms like Facebook and you end up seeing it. Now that we can see how much distraction is all around, all the time, how can we cut through it and focus on building wealth through property.

Being totally focused on one thing at a time helps so working in short time slots with no distractions can be of benefit. Switch off the updates or notifications on your computer, laptop, tablet or smartphone. If you still carry an old Nokia phone you might be OK.

Meditation is extremely useful for helping your state of mind. When you are relaxed and giving your attention on the present then you are going to be focused on the job in hand. Don't try to multi-task as your mind wanders between tasks and is likely to wander towards other things such as, what you've got planned for the weekend. Getting in the right frame of mind before starting very important tasks is vital if you want to get the best possible outcome. Clearing your mind beforehand is a big help. We mentioned meditation and how that can help, as can listening to music.

Different types of music can be used to get you "in the zone" for different types of focus. Sports men and women may use loud "pumping music" to get themselves psyched up before an event. Public speakers may listen to relation music before a speaking gig. As well as music we have met "speakers" who use small indoor trampolines to jump up and down to get themselves energized before a talk. Another way to relax is to stop listening to that voice in your head. It's called your monkey mind and its constantly chatting away to you, asking you things like, did I forget to call someone? Was I supposed to do something for someone? Was I supposed to be somewhere? Do I look OK? Was that person looking at me? Or did I do OK? This voice never stops, and it gets in the way of being totally focused. I've found that one way of helping to stop this constant voice is to use a journal, a reminder or to-do list and/or a planner. That way you can dump the overload from your mind, clearing your thoughts to help you focus better. keeping a journal is extremely useful for several reasons. Firstly, it helps you clear the clutter from your mind. Secondly, it helps you reflect on what's happened in your life, the challenges and the successes and how you dealt with them. Keeping a journal also helps to show you how you felt at particular times and it therefore becomes a point of reference. You can use your journal to look back and remember how you dealt with challenges in the past so that you can now focus on getting a better outcome in the future. This frees up time to deal with other important tasks. There are many great books out there that help you to "journal" including 365 Journal Writing Ideas by Rossi Fox. This book has a small journaling task to complete day that helps you focus on one particular thing. It also has a list of photographs for you to take including landscapes, animals, flowers, flags, scenery and several other things. Not only does this help you focus on looking out for these things, but it helps you to appreciate the world around you, being more present, observant and aware of the beauty of nature. You also become more appreciative, more self reflecting, creative, more goal orientated with a definitive sense of direction and definitely more focused. Speaking from a personal experience, journaling works.

You Always Have Two Choices:
Your Commitment Versus
Your Fear"

Sammy Davis Jr.

Chapter 5

Setting Yourself Up for Success
This chapter is all about YOU.

> *"We can have more than we've got because we can become more than we are"*
>
> **Jim Rohn**

Before you start any project including your property investing projects, you need to be clear about what you want, and more importantly, why you want it.

Firstly, if you don't know what you want then how will you know when you've got it. We have encountered so many people with sizeable property portfolios with good income who aren't happy or content because they really don't know what they want, and if they do then they don't know why they want it. They start out with a target of 5 properties, then it becomes 10, then 20, then 30 and so on. They become focused on the number of properties and the amount of income they want rather than what kind of lifestyle that it can provide. They get caught up in their own game of adding more and more properties to their portfolio and more and more money to their bank accounts, yet they don't enjoy the benefits of it because they don't know why they want it. They like the sound of having a huge portfolio and lots of money but still live like they had nothing. They don't reward themselves.

Just think for a moment and ask yourself some more questions?

- ❐ Why am I investing in property or why am I thinking about doing it?

- ❐ Why do I get up early each morning, commute to work and spend a huge chunk of my life making someone else wealthy? Is it for wages alone or is it because the wages feed and clothe me and my family, pay for cars, holidays, hobbies, pets, saving for a rainy day or kids' college or university fees.

Whatever the reason, the **WHY** is stronger than the **WHAT**. If your **WHY** wasn't stronger then the **WHAT**, then you wouldn't go to work at all. The desire would disappear and you would become unhappy. When your why is stronger than the how or the what then you have more clarity and more focus. Your why gives you the driving force and motivation.

When it comes to goal setting you should firstly focus on the why. If you have a thought in your head such as "I'd like to quit my job" ask yourself why you like this would to become reality. Is it to spend more time with family and friends and if so, why? Is it to spend more time travelling and if so, with whom, where to and why? Do you just want to be financially free? When you focus on gaining clarity as to why you want something so much then it's going to push you to take action towards achieving that goal. Once you have a strong why for your goals, you need to write them down and start to put together an action plan to help you achieve them. You should do that right away. Don't put it off any longer.

In order to help you plan your goals you may want to use the **SMART** formula for goal setting.

> **Specific** – (simple, sensible, significant)
>
> **Measurable** – (meaningful, motivating)
>
> **Achievable** – (agreed, attainable)
>
> **Relevant** – (reasonable, realistic, resourced)
>
> **Time Bound** - (time based, time cost, time sensitive

Specific - Your goals should be crystal clear otherwise you won't be able to focus your efforts or feel motivated enough. Try answering the following 5 questions.

❐ What do I want to accomplish?

❐ Why is it so important?

❐ Who is involved?

❐ Where is it located?

❐ Which resources or limits are involved?

Imagine you are starting off as a new investor and want to earn enough money to quit your job. Your goals might look something like this.

❐ I want to earn £X per month (X equals your current take home pay)

❐ This goal is important to me because it gives me time freedom, it means I can stop being a wage slave and have control over my own future.

❐ My Powerteam includes (list all the people whose help you need) will be involved in helping me achieve this goal. I will meet person A every 2 weeks, person B x1 per month, person C as required.

❐ I will invest in Belfast, London, Dublin, Glasgow, Cardiff or wherever it is you want to invest or even a combination of these places.

❐ I will need £50,000 to get started. I will need a Powerteam, I will need a mentor, I will need to learn some property investment strategies. I will be restricted by mortgage rules regarding refinancing or any other restriction (take advice)

Measurable- Instead of saying "I want enough money to quit my job" say I want to replace my £2000 take home pay.

Achievable - Can I go out and achieve this goal? Do I have a good credit? Will I be able to raise the finance necessary to get started? If not, can I find enough Joint Venture partners or Angel Investment Funders to fund my project. Do I have the right Powerteam around me to help achieve my goal? Can I achieve my goal in the time- frame that I've set?

Realistic - Am I being realistic with my goals? If I set big targets have I given myself enough time? Ten properties within one year might be achievable whereas fifty properties might not unless you have an endless supply of cash.

Timebound - I need to set a time-frame for my goals otherwise there will be no urgency or no deadlines to meet. My goals will most likely just run and run, and I will lose momentum and those goals will fade away. Setting a time-frame could be as simple as viewing ten properties per week, making offers on five, purchasing one and completing a refurbishment within 4 months. Having weekly, monthly, quarterly, half yearly and yearly targets helps to keep things in a time frame.

A SMART goal always has a time frame.

Another important aspect of goal setting is to include some form of accountability. Find someone you trust who will support you but also be open and honest if you aren't making the grade. When someone else knows you have a goal and that it has a deadline then this gives some bite to the process. If you are the only person who knows then your goals might not have as much power and it is definitely more powerful if someone can keep you accountable and support you at times when you are experiencing some challenges. So, what are you waiting for? Go set yourself some big goals, goals that inspire you, goals that challenge you and not small goals that are easily achieved. Set some big ass goals that, even if you fail and achieve only 50% of your target will still represent a huge progress on where you started. If your goals, the ones you have written down with a plan, don't challenge you then can I suggest that your first goal should be to get skilled at setting some big ass goals. Forget about what everyone else wants for a second and set goals that are all about you and the things that matter to you. That might sound a bit selfish, but you need to think about fitting your own oxygen mask before helping others.

Goal setting is important, in fact, it's extremely important because it challenges you and helps you to grow and if you're not growing then you're dying. To reach the next level you need to grow and it's that simple.

So, let's say you have set yourself 5 key goals in areas of your life that really matter. They can be from the following; Finances, Business/ Career, Family, Relationships, Spiritual, Learning or Health & Fitness. Then what next? Don't be one of those people who lives on Someday Isle. The one's you hear saying, someday

I'll do this and someday I'll do that. You need to take action. You need to start today. Not tomorrow, not next week, not next month, not next year. Why? Because there's no time like the present to get started. If you don't then this time next year, you'll be wishing you'd started today. Jim Rohn says the time to act is when the idea is hot, and the emotion is strong so act before the feeling passes. Do it now, carry a notebook or use the voice recorder on your smartphone and put it to good use. Take action immediately. If you don't then the intent diminishes. Take action immediately with discipline because your goals should matter to you and you will only achieve them by taking consistent, disciplined action, every day. Even small amounts of consistent, disciplined action is all about change. Unfortunately change is a scary word for some people. Some people are scared to change in case others don't approve of them because they appear different and being different makes them feel uncomfortable. Especially when being judged by others. You can have absolutely anything you want in life, *you can have more, if you become more.* If **you** change then things around you start to change. We all wish for an easy life, but you will need to become a stronger, better and more intelligent person for things to seem easier. Just take a moment to think about how changing can impact on your life. What if I was stronger, wiser, more confident, calmer, a better parent, spouse, partner, brother, sister etc. How would this affect your life. How could this then have a positive effect on others. If you help yourself then how many other people could you help? If you were a better parent would your children be better? If you were a better boss or co-worker would your employee's or colleagues be better? The answer is probably yes. You become an attractive character which can attract other positive, like-minded people and bring greater opportunities. When you become a better, stronger and more confident person, opportunities seem to come to you instead of you always seeking them. Here are some tips on becoming a better, stronger and wiser person.

- ❑ Read as much as you can. Read or listen to personal development, investment and business books. I recommend Jim Rohn for personal development but there are many others. You can watch tons of personal development videos on You Tube and many PDF books and eBooks are available online for free.

- ❑ Keep a journal. I mentioned the benefits of journaling in chapter 4 and I personally believe that it is so important that I will cover it again. keeping a journal is much more than keeping a diary. Life happens to us very quickly. As the old saying goes, "life just seems to pass us by". We seldom have time to think about it. Journaling is a great way to record experiences, challenges, special moments, good times and sad times. A journal becomes a permanent log of everything, your idea's thoughts, events, challenges, memories and anything else worth remembering. Even sometimes recording the things you'd rather forget about can be useful when looking back at how dealt with that particular issue. Journaling is also a great way to check your personal development progress. You can check back to see how you dealt with challenges in the past and see if certain things that used to be a challenge are now not viewed as such. Previous challenges are now routine events. Your journal also becomes a personal reference guide to the past and as I mentioned earlier it's a great tool to dump the contents of your mind, to download, to filter events and feelings and store them for the future. You should also use your journal to record your goals and monitor their progress. Your grammar, spelling, hand-writing and writing speed should also improve the more you journal which is something that is lost in today's technology era. There are no rules to writing your journal except the rules you want to abide by, if any. In my journal I have a couple of envelopes glued to the inside front and back covers to keep ticket stubs, some receipts, photos and any other bits and pieces I think are worthy of keeping. I also have a list of photographs to take which I tick off as I go. They are random photos such a scenery, landmarks or landscapes, different coloured items, street art, portraits and many other things. I didn't quite get it at first, but I now understand the need to be present in the now and appreciate what's around me.

With each photograph I have something extra to write about and an extra dimension to my memories. It's all about my personal awareness and appreciation. Why not give it a go and see if it works for you?

"What you get by achieving your goals is not as important as what you become by achieving your goals"

ZIG ZIGLAR

Chapter 6

Strategies. What Strategies?

> *"A vision without a strategy remains an illusion"*
>
> **Lee Bolman**

When we began to invest in property back in 2005 we had no idea what "property investing strategies" were. You bought a property and waited for the price to go up or you bought a fixer upper, refurbished it and sold on for profit. We had no idea how many different ways there was to make money from property. We were totally oblivious to the fact that you could make money by controlling property using some legal paperwork or agreements. How was this even possible? Surely you had to buy property to buy property to make money. You needed to have money to make money? Right?. Wrong, and how wrong we were.

In 2008 when the property crash hit The Uk & Ireland, Northern Ireland was one of the worst affected areas. Prices had risen so fast in the few years prior to the crash, that when the crash happened, prices tumbled to about 1/3 or less of their peak values in some cases. We were highly leveraged at that point and found it difficult to get more mortgages at a time when property was "dirt cheap". We needed mortgages more than ever, but that option was no longer available. We had credit card and personal loan debt like many other people and we were shifting the debt between 0% interest credit cards and paying it down quickly. Then, BOOM! Our credit rating took a hit because of some poor choices we made and by taking our eye of the ball. We had used credit cards to fund the deposit for a property in Egypt which never materialized. That was a £22,000 lesson. The company had gone bust and the cost of trying to get the money was risky because there was a chance it could cost us loads more for no return. We decided to let it go. We had also paid some reservation fees to property sourcing companies both in England and Spain which for one reason or another never came to fruition. This was a tough period in our lives and lead to a lot of questioning of whether we had done the right thing in getting involved in property investing in the first place. You would expect that, because we had our fingers burnt so badly that we would have walked away. I had given up my job in the Merchant Navy at that point. When the crash happened, the Bank of England reduced the interest rates and because our most of our mortgages were on Bank Base Rate (BBR) + X %, most of our mortgage payments dropped dramatically. On one particular property the mortgage dropped to five pence per month. Yes, 5p per month with rental income of £475, management fees of £47.50 and insurance of £15. We were cash flowing £412.50 per month on just one property.

Instead of being scared of having had our fingers burnt so badly and being left with all the credit card debt and no 0% payment option we decided not to give up but to battle on. We invested heavily in ourselves which was by far and away the best investment we ever made. As Benjamin Franklin claimed **"An investment in knowledge pays the best interest"**

We had no choice but to invest in ourselves. As I have already mentioned at the beginning of this chapter, Northern Ireland was suffering a serious property downturn and most investors had run for the hills, which all of sudden left loads of property on the market at very cheap prices. For most people the thought of investing about £20,000 in property education seemed total madness. We have spent more than double that since 2008 in various trainings, seminars, workshops, books, CD's, DVD's, memberships and coaching. Mostly based in England, there was also the added cost of travel and accommodation for 3, 4 or 5 nights away. The single biggest benefit for us in this investment was the shift away from buying whatever house was offered. We now only bought properties below market value that we could add value to, then refinance to recycle our cash or our JV partners cash. This meant we could repeat the process over and over again.

Due to our credit status we were now forced to buy for cash using JV partners money or buy using "mortgage hosts". When your back is against the wall you become determined to find solutions to your problems in order to be successful. We had good cashflow due to mortgage rates falling but it was around this time that I had been thinking about leaving my job in the Merchant Navy and working as a Full Time Property Investor. It was a very big decision, but I made the decision with a little bit of fear. Fear that things might not turn out the way I wanted them to.

In my last Merchant Navy job, I had my travel expenses paid, all my meals and although not a huge salary it qualified for Merchant Seafarers Tax Status. This meant that if I was out of the Uk more days than I was in the Uk I wouldn't have to pay income tax. I gave the job up in May 2009 and immediately started in a property management business with 3 other partners who were also running a mortgage business. I had got some qualifications in Energy Performance Certificates which brought some more income. The property management business didn't seem to be going anywhere and I was keen to do my own thing, so I left and went out on my own. I started a business working from home and it was during this time that I started to focus on doing joint ventures with other investors. I had the knowledge, skills and time and had learned to leverage other people's money from what we had been taught at the property investing seminars.

The number one thing that we got from our initial investment in education was the network of people we built up was the network of people from all across the Uk. People like Lindsay Hopkins who has since become a friend and mentor, who believed in us when things were tough, who gave us much valuable information and who also came to speak on several occasions at our network event, The Belfast Property Meet. Lindsay has given us some great words of advice over the years none more so that "find a good deal and money will come to the deal". We also give credit to Lindsay for helping us move from small projects to bigger projects which opened our minds to what possibilities were available under our noses. Another person who has been a huge influence in our lives both personally and in business, is Brian Muldoon. Without Brian's wisdom and great advice, we wouldn't have got Property Success University off the ground nor would we have written this book. Both would have remained "on the drawing board".

"When your headlights aren't on, the best rear-view mirror available isn't likely to improve your driving"

MARTH ROGERS

Chapter 7

Being Fearful v Being Greedy

> *"Be fearful when others are being greedy and be greedy when others are being fearful"*
>
> ***Warren Buffett***

One of the other reasons why it's important to invest in yourself is that you will have the ability to do your own thing. You won't have to follow the crowd any longer. You won't have to invest in property with huge sums of your own money and wait for the price to go up as the only way to make decent money. You won't become one of the many people who become casualties of the property cycles because they thought prices would just keep rising. Unfortunately, a lot of people got their fingers burnt in 2008 as they bought high and expected prices to just keep rising.

Unfortunately, the same thing will happen again as some people will not have learned the lessons of the previous crash. Don't get me wrong, many people made lots of money but lots of people got caught up in the frenzy of rising prices and didn't know when to stop. Fortunately for you, a property education will help you spot the opportunities and avoid the pitfalls. In my experience, the people who got caught were developers and smaller investors who bought land and built big detached properties. Once the bubble burst the value of land dropped like a stone and these small, medium and big time developers were left with land valued at less than half of what they paid for it, The other problem was that the banks had dramatically reduced their lending, or in most cases stopped lending, so these developers couldn't borrow money to fund their projects. Developers who had been selling detached properties for £250,000-£300,000 and more now found themselves going under with banks repossessing sites and properties. The banks then started selling them off at auctions for around £100,000 or if they were unfinished, sometimes a lot less. Warren Buffet, the great stock market investor has a great quote which I used as the opening quote in this chapter. "Be fearful when others are being greedy and be greedy when others are being fearful. From the start of the crash in 2008 to 2012 when properties hit the bottom of the cycle most property investors had stopped buying.

Properties in our area, the 2-3 bedroom terraced houses that were all the rage before 2008, had been selling for £120,000 plus. They were now selling for £30,000-£40,000. I talked to a lot of people back in 2011-12 who were concerned that property prices had fallen so much, and most were happy to wait until the market changed before they would consider buying again. At the time I remember thinking that it was strange that people didn't want to buy cheap property and were happy to wait until the prices went back up. Surely the yields of 15-20% were enough to attract even the most amateur investor but apparently not. Even if you bought a property that needed refurbished, the yields were still 10% + and return on cash invested was in excess of 20%. It was a "no brainer" for us but for many others "it wasn't the right time to buy". The others were probably waiting for the media to report that it was "the right time". By that time the real value would be gone and every man and his dog and the next door neighbours' dog would be piling back in again and the frenzy would start all over again. So, avoid the sheep. Look at the masses and do the opposite. We always focused on 2, 3 and 4 bedroom properties in areas where there is high rental demand. We have always avoided higher priced properties such as semi's or detached houses be-cause they are more expensive to buy and proportionally do not bring in as much rent as the cheaper properties. Their yields are lower and more importantly their return on cash invested is much lower. A typical 3 bed terrace would achieve £500 per month whereas a 3 bed semi or 3 bed detached may only get £600 per month. Here are some comparisons between the ter-raced properties and the detached properties based on a purchase price of £70,000 for a 3 bed terrace and £140,000 for a 3 bed detached.

Property A	Property B
3 bed terrace	3 bed detached
(Yield)	*(Yield)*
Rent £500 pcm/£6,000 p.a.	Rent £600 pcm £7,200
Yield £6,000/£70,000 **8.5%**	Yield £7,200/£140,000 **5.1%**
(Return on cash invested)	**(Return on cash invested)**
Deposit £17,500 (25%)	Deposit £35,000
Rent £6,000	Rent £7,200
R.O.C.I. £6000/£17500 **34%**	R.O.C.I. £7200/£35000 **20.5%**

These figures do not take into account other purchase or monthly mortgage costs, but it gives you an idea of the returns. If both properties were purchased using a 25% deposit, then we can see the cash flow for both in the following example. Let's assume we are using an interest only mortgage at an interest rate of 2.5% which was typical at the time of writing.

Property A		Property B	
Price	£70,000	Price	£140,000
Deposit	£17,500	Deposit	£35,000
Mortgage	£52,500	Mortgage	£105,000
Payment	£109.38	Payment	£218.75
Rent	£500.00	Rent	£600.00
Insurance	£20.00	Insurance	£25.00
Cash Flow	£370.62	Cash Flow	£356.25

As you can see the investment for Property B has a cash investment of £35,000 and a cash flow of £356.25 per month or £4275 per year which is a 12.2% return on cash invested.

Property A, on the other hand, has a cash flow of £370.62 per month or £4440 per year for an outlay of £17,500 which is 25.4% return on cash invested.

The other purchase costs to consider are the different rates of stamp duty land tax (SDLT) on both properties. (3% on everything if a property costs £40,000 or more and 2% on everything above £125,000). For Property A the SDLT would be £2,100 on Property A and £4,500 (£4,200 + £300) on Property B. This increase in purchase costs therefore reduces the return on cash invested more so on the higher priced property. (Property B)

Here's something to think about. What if you don't have the initial £17,500 plus closing or purchase costs. Do you have a relative who might have some money sitting in their bank account earning 1% interest or less? (When you take inflation into account of 2.5% plus, then they are actually losing money). Could you offer them 5, 6 or 7% per annum on the same sum of money and/or an equity share in a property? You could get the mortgage, they put in the deposit (ask a mortgage advisor how to structure this). You then ask your solicitor to draw up a Deed of Trust for both parties for your share in the property. You then pay your relative the interest on their investment and the percentage share of any profit. They would also benefit from any share of capital growth that may occur when you come to sell the property. Do whatever works best for both parties, provided you both make a good return. We have used this strategy on numerous occasions and it is still working well for us.

Remember, when your back is against the wall, you become quite resilient and are able to come up with solutions to various problems, or challenges, as you should call them from now on.

Another strategy that has worked extremely well for us is Assisted Sales. When you can't get mortgages due to being maxed out or not having the required credit status, Assisted Sales can be a life saver. You also don't have to worry about finding huge sums of money for deposits and stamp duty. We initially used this strategy to help someone we met who has several properties that were empty, needed some refurbishment but they didn't have the spare capital to pay for the work. They were asset rich but cash poor.

Here's the first example of an assisted sale that worked out fairly good for us but also had some lessons along the way. The property was an ex local authority 3 bed mid terrace, which had been empty for several years and was in poor condition. The previous tenants had kept a big dog in the house and it smelt pretty bad. The gardens were overgrown and a huge tree at the front had grown so much that some of its branches were leaning on the roof. The kitchen was in poor state and there was ivy growing up the back walls so bad that the kitchen and bathroom windows couldn't be opened. The boiler had been stolen and the front door panels had been kicked in. The property looked in really bad condition but once the clear out was complete it would look different and not as bad as we first thought. It needed a new boiler, new kitchen and bathroom then the usual cosmetics such as new tiles, new flooring, new carpets and repainted. The owner had initially suggested putting the property though an auction for £40,000. With auction fees to be deducted and most lots not making their list price at that time we knew that we could possibly offer the owner more for the property on an assisted sale agreement. We could then refurbish it and sell it for profit. We agreed an assisted sale price of £45,000. This would mean the owner got more with less costs and we wouldn't have to put down a 25% deposit at best or if not mortgageable, then the full £45,000 plus refurbishment costs. We drew up three documents with our solicitor. The first document outlined the details of the deal including the agreed price, the rough outline of refurbishment work, permission to market the property on completion of works and other caveats including us not being allowed to move in or rent the property without the owner's permission.

The second document was a caretaker's agreement which gave us permission as "caretakers owners" to carry out any work that we thought was reasonable to get the property into a sellable condition. The third document was a legal charge on the title which would be registered at Land Registry. We agreed that we would spend approximately £12,000 - £15,000 so we put a charge on for £25,000 to protect our expenditure and some level of future profit. We got to work within a few days. So, no forking out £45,000 to purchase the property and no waiting for a whole purchase transaction to take place. The title was checked by our solicitor who then told us that we were good to go on the refurbishment.

We placed a builders skip in the front garden and got started. At the time of this project we hadn't fully appreciated the term "Leverage". We thought that by doing the clearing out work ourselves that we would save money, which I suppose we did but we wasted loads more time than if we'd paid someone else to do the work. We were trying to fit this project around running a small letting agency as we as other family matters such as collecting our daughter from school 25 miles away from the project. As you can imagine the project took longer than we anticipated and because we paid for materials and other costs with whatever money we had, that added more time trying to get funds together. When we look back we realize that we should have leveraged other people's time and money to get the job done quicker. We would have had slightly less profit but would have saved a few months on the work which market, got some enquiries and agreed a sale to a first time would have allowed us to move on to the next project far quicker. Despite the slow process we got the job done and got the property on the buyer couple for £72,000 within 2 weeks. We had to pay the owner £45,000 on completion of the sale and we would keep anything over £45,000. We got the £27,000 difference so we made a profit of £15,000 having spent £12,000 on the work. So, we invested £12,000 and got back £27,000, a profit of 125%. As I mentioned we should have leveraged more. We could have paid someone else to do the "dirty work" and used funds from an investor and completed the project in 8 weeks instead of 5 months. Less profit but moving to the next project in a far quicker time. The next project and each one moving forward would involve as much leverage as possible. That was a huge learning curve as we realised that the biggest leverage aspect was 'time'. We can always get more money, but we can never get more time. The next project, a similar property type, took about 3 months with lots more work, more leverage but less profit. We invested £19,000 and made £12,000 profit but in a much quicker time So, you can clearly see the benefits of doing assisted sales. If you are getting started and don't have lots of funds, then this strategy is a winner. No mortgages, no deposits and no long drawn out purchase process before you get started. As I mentioned in the example, finding a friend or family member who might have savings and earning poor interest can be the secret to making these deals work. If you are on hand to project manage while someone else funds these deals you can make good money quickly for both you and the property owner while at the same time giving your investor good interest rates.

If we had paid 1% per month on £12,000 for 5 months our first assisted sale we would have would still have made £14,400 profit instead of £15,000 as we would have paid £120 per month (1%), a total of £600 over 5 months. If you think that wouldn't work, then consider offering more. 1% per month is a lot better than 1% per annum in the savings account. If you paid £1000 in interest for 5 months you would still walk away with £14,000 pretax profit.

Once you find someone who is happy to get good returns on their savings and they invest in a successful project then the chances are they are likely to come back for more, even waiting patiently for your next project. Many savers are just like you, in that they want more out of life but unlike you they haven't got the skills or knowledge to use their money to get the kind of returns that you can. They play it safe until someone like you can show them fairly risk free way to make more money. You will have presented them with an investment plan showing your project, your due diligence, the numbers, the costs and your exit strategy. In other words, the what, the where, the how and the when you intend to pay them back their money plus interest. In Chapter 2 we discussed about the importance of building relationships. When we began doing assisted sales and involving other investors we were oblivious to how important the relationships would be. By giving investors a good return, then having the opportunity to talk about how we did those deals to other investors at network events, it opened up many doors for us. Getting up to present those deals in front of others at network events is scary at first but it really is pure gold. You gain credibility being at the front of the room, you gain an expert status and you just might find investors for future deals. If you don't fancy the idea of speaking in front of others, then that's OK but this property investing business is all about stepping outside your comfort zone so take the opportunity to speak up and seize the opportunities that are waiting for you. The more you step out of your comfort zone, the more rewards will come your way.

"Real estate investing, even on a
very small scale, remains a tried
and true means of building
an individual's cash flow
and wealth"

ROBERT KIYOSAKI

Chapter 8

Closing the Deal

> *"Life begins at the end of your comfort zone"*
>
> **Neale Donald Walsch**

So the skills that we developed over a few short years helped us get the big deal over the line. There were many challenges to over-come throughout the project, but we overcame them all because we were determined we were going to succeed. We were focused on succeeding instead of being focused on "not losing" as most people tend to be these days. Whether we had developed this skill by accident or whether it happened due to a combination of failing more than once, followed by huge learning, is open to debate but having made those mistakes we learned lessons, sharpened our skills and moved onto the next project with less fear than the previous one.

The big deal in question was a block of six apartments in run down condition which we secured using some bridging finance and some investor finance. We were on holidays at a friend's wedding in Ibiza when the completion took place. On our return from Ibiza the work got under way. The renovation got under way, firstly by stripping the apartments back to the brick and removing all stud walls. Then we completed any remedial works before any of the serious work began. The other work involved was finding more investment funds and this was ongoing throughout the project. We had a friend who was speaking at our network event and she introduced us to a friend who made a £50,000 investment. Around the same time, we found another £50,000 investor through one of the existing investors. As Christmas approached we were very low on funds. We had to wait on the £100k of investment to be paid via our solicitor but his office was now closed for the holiday period. The agreements that the investors signed had been delayed in the "Christmas Post" so we had to wait until the New Year. With just 2 days before the break, we managed to secure £20,000 of funds to keep the project moving. It was a scary time, a time when we thought things we going against us but we kept going and kept believing that everything would work out. One of the things that worked in our favour was having an account with a local builder's merchant with 60 days credit. We used that to our advantage. By early 2016 the project was taking shape. Things were frantic inside with labourers, joiners, plumbers, electricians falling over each other. By early February the top floor apartments were starting nearing completion. We had planned to finish from the top down. The scaffolding had been removed from the front of the property to expose the new pointed front, the new PVC sash windows and some new sandstone window heads so the appearance from the street had changed dramatically. Towards the middle of February, we faced another challenge when some men walked off the job after a dispute with the project manager. Where on earth would we find decent tradesmen at such short notice to finish off the project? We kept focused. We kept our eyes on the prize and were determined to make it happen. The two top floor apartments were ready by the end February and we had already sold them off market. One of our investors introduced us to a cash buyer who wanted to buy an apartment in that area because of its proximity to Queens University. The second buyer was a JV partner of ours in other properties. We struck a deal on the second apartment on a JV basis with the investor. That left 4 of the 6 apartments to go to the open market with a local agent. They had marketed the properties using some computerized images prior to completion of the works to drum up interest.

During the initial marketing campaign, we still needed to find some funds to finish the lower floor apartment and front and rear gardens. We had initially estimated spending around £30,000 per unit but it ended up being £45,000 per unit due to the quality of our kitchens, integrated white goods, bathrooms, PVC sash windows instead of standard PVC windows, and the addition of a wall with wrought iron railings to the front.

Some of the other costs that we didn't consider or found hard to estimate was the pointing and the cost of scaffolding as it was hard to pin down how long the scaffolding would be in place for. As it is charged by the week, the cost of it was double what we had planned for, purely because the pointing was a slow job.

When we did some comparable pricing at the outset we came across 1 and 2 bed apartments on a street nearby for between £100,000 and £120,000. With 4 x 2 bed and 2 x 1 bed this would give us an end value of £650,000 - £680,000. Our apartments were located in a more sought after street so as the project developed we were able to capitalize on the market conditions, go for better quality fixtures and fittings and then market them at higher prices. The demand was there so why not. When we bought the block in September 2015 there were other empty properties on the same street that had been bought for huge sums of money before the crash but ended up lying empty for a few years. By the time we had finished the project in March 2016 many of the other empty properties on the street were now being converted into luxury apartments. By finishing in mid-March, we had been on site for just short of 6 months. We had to borrow a small sum of money from friends and family to finish the job. One of our friends got a loan at around 5% and lent it to us for a lot more and made a profit from someone else's money. How's that for leverage?

We had offered very good returns to our investors because at 10% some people wouldn't be interested, at 12% they showed interest but at 15% it was a no brainer. Once we presented a business plan and answered questions about security, loan agreements, payback time, late fees etc. then most of the people we spoke to we keen to invest. That's a big part of the formula for attracting investors. If you offer a sizable return, then you make it easier for them to say yes.

As we were getting towards the end of the project, I had attended a network event where one of the speakers was talking about "serviced accommodation". We had attempted holiday lets a few years earlier in Portrush, a popular seaside town in County Antrim. That was back in 2010 when we didn't know how to leverage. The whole idea seemed too much like hard word as we checked in our guests in person, did the cleaning and laundry ourselves and didn't have the luxury of Airbnb or Booking.com.

Serviced Accommodation units (SAC) were becoming very popular and after having a conversation with one of my JV partners we agreed to give it a go. Within a few weeks we had our first SAC unit up and running. A visit to a Swedish Furniture store with a van saw us purchase most of what we needed to get things going.

So here we were, still finishing the biggest project we'd ever taken on and we were adding "serviced accommodation" hosts to our list of property based business ventures. We also owned a Property Management business, ran a monthly property network event as well as coaching and mentoring some new property investors.

During the next few months of 2016 we had the other four apartments sale agreed. One of those fell through after 4 months of time wasting with one of the others being purchased by another JV partner. In early July we had 3 serviced units running, two with JV partners and the other being managed for the cash buyer who wanted an apartment near Queens University.

The renovation of the 6 apartments was well and truly complete and the placed looked amazing. (See the pictures below and judge for yourself)

We were really proud of the completed product. In early August, three of the sales had gone through. We were able to pay back the bridging company and the first few investors. The investors were paid back based on their level of security i.e. first or second charge and then on their entry point i.e. first in, first out. Two other apartments completed in the next 6-8 weeks and we were home and hosed. All investors had been paid back including interest and the last property would be the bulk of our profit. The deal that fell through was again considered a possibility as another serviced unit. The occupancy for the others was very good so it was an opportunity to JV once again. **By the end of this great project we had generated** £150,000 **using none of our own money.** When you consider the returns that we had given to investors it could have been a lot more. But here's the key to using other people's money. If you make a profit using other people's money then your return is 'infinite' it's not 10%, not 50% and not 100%. Its infinite. By leveraging other people's money, albeit at an extremely good rate for investors, we were able to learn some massive lessons. We had to overcome some great challenges, win the confidence of more investors and this helped us walk away with £150,000 using none of our own money. Not only that but we now had four serviced units under our management, three of which we had a fifty percent share of price plus a management fee. We still get a tremendous sense of pride each time we see these apartments. It was the catalyst for other work to start on the street as other developers started work as our project came to an end. The street has all manner of luxury apartments springing up and the serviced accommodation we offer in that street is very popular with some corporate guests.

"As you move outside your comfort, what was once the unknown and frightening becomes your new normal"

ROBIN S SHARMA

Chapter 9

The Future and You

> "The two greatest fear busters are knowledge and action"
>
> **Denis Waitley**

We hope that you can now see that, with the right knowledge and the right action, the right results are possible. We grew up in working class families, semi-skilled or farmers and had no family wealth around us. Everything in life happens for a reason and usually when things don't go according to plan you decide its time to stop. You give up because you don't want things to go wrong again. You shouldn't give up. Keep going and learn the lessons from things that go wrong. Those lessons make you stronger.

For a few years Mary had planned to give up work. I gave up my life in the Merchant Navy in 2009 and made the tough decision to focus on property. Within a few months our credit rating tumbled, and our backs were against the wall. We reacted positively to this set back and it helped us become resourceful, thinking outside the box types, helping others as well as ourselves. We adopted an open, outward thinking attitude which helped us build relationships. We have a number of JV partners and we are constantly looking to build relationships with others. You may not see the value in this just yet but trust in yourself and build as many relationships as you can.

You must also learn to trust your gut when it comes to other people. If something doesn't feel just right, then move on. We have come across many fly by nights, out to make a quick buck and then disappear faster than they appeared. You know the types, we've all met them, it's all about them, problems are never their fault, in fact they tend to disappear at the first sign of a problem, won't return your calls, texts or emails. They leave the problem solving for others to sort out. Avoid these types like the plague but if you only realise when you're in a deal then make sure legal paperwork is water tight and covers everything. A good solicitor is worth every penny and we are lucky that we have one. Your solicitor is a vital part of your Powerteam.

You need a number of people in your Powerteam including a good mortgage broker, (get one who is also a property investor) a handyman, tradesmen, a letting agent, an estate agent, a coach or mentor and an accountant. For us the solicitor is usually the first port of call and the person who protects your legal interest in anything. Most building problems can be fixed quite easily but most legal problems can be costly so get a good solicitor. An accountant, who understands your property business and saves you money is also a must. Handymen and tradesmen tend to come and go, and you will most likely go through quite a few before you get someone reliable and value for money. It has taken us a number of years and some tough lessons.

Back in 2016 Mary had finally decided to give up work but when it came to actually 'doing it' it was a different story. Mary had been part of other peoples Powerteams. She had been coaching and mentoring and generally being available to help out or advise her coaching clients or mentees. The thing that she found out most from them was that many of them wanted to give up work, especially the middle income earners in fairly good careers, but the thing that held them back was fear. This spurred Mary on and after a few false alarms, where she wanted to hand in her notice but couldn't quite do it she finally took the plunge in June 2016.

The second biggest fear of most people after quitting their job was having nothing to do once they'd quit their job. Believe me, when you get into property investing and commit to improving yourself as a person you will never be bored. There is so much to do and so much will happen that you'll wonder how you managed to squeeze in 40-50 hours per week working and commuting to work. I honestly can't remember the last time I felt bored. I have so much growing, learning and developing to do. We also have businesses to build.

Each part of our business started as an idea as did every other business at some point. The reason why we had a good level of success is down to taking action. That one thing that can make a huge difference. If you don't take action, you don't get results. If you don't fire then you won't hit the target, if you don't ask then the answer will always be no and if you don't change then things will stay the same. Physically we stop growing in our teenage years but mentally we, should never stop growing. The difference between older people who look years younger and those who don't is often down to how active they are not just physically but mentally. What is the one thing, the one action you can take right away to help you grow and develop as a person. A journey of a thousand miles starts with a small step. What's your small step?

> "You don't have to be great to start, but you have to start to be great"
>
> **ZIG ZIGLAR**

Chapter 10

Conclusion

We hope you found this book useful and if you've got this far then I'd like to congratulate you. We've tried to keep this as uncomplicated as possible to let you draw your own conclusions, to take a step back and think of where you're coming from and where you are heading to? Most people don't. They're like ships. There's someone in the wheelhouse but no one's controlling the wheel. If there's no plan, then you won't know if you're veering off course and if you don't know what you want and why you want it how will you know when you've achieved it. I can't emphasize enough how important education is but for me and Mary, it has to be the right kind of education. Jim Rohn's quote sums it up nicely, " Formal education will make you a living; self education will make you a fortune"

You can see throughout this book that the more action we took the more success we had. Who knows, if we had taken more action we'd most likely have more success, and I believe that you can do the same. If you have found this book useful or inspiring, then we'd like to hear from you. Please drop us an email with your feedback to support@ propertysuccessuniversity.com.

If you would like to speak to us directly or take part in our monthly membership platform, then please go to

www.PropertySuccessUniversity.com

Here's What Some of Our Existing Members Have to Say

Last year I met some people who changed my life completely, who help me to see the world from the different perspective, who has shared with me the key to the success. This opened the door to a property journey. I joined Property Success University's online membership and it has given me an incredible opportunity to change my mindset and learn property investing strategies that I wasn't aware before. Within a few months I raised over £100,000 in finance and purchased my first 5 bed multi let investment property. Currently, this property gives me an annual reoccurring income which is more than is the minimum wage in the UK. I have to say, it wasn't easy and few times I was close to giving up, but it was worth the effort and the challenges I faced are now behind me. I would like to take this opportunity to say thank you to Mary and Chris, my friends and my business mentors as I wouldn't be here without them

Sebastian Rogala

Chris and Mary have a great passion for property, fantastic knowledge and they are true example of people who are honest, hard working, inspirational, and very kind that is so hard to meet nowadays. They put me on the fast track with my property journey to become more successful, better all round person.

Lucas Kowalczyk

I had dabbled in property in the past but it hadn't went well. I had lost confidence in my decision making due to bad purchases. Mary & Chris have, through PSU and being part of my Powerteam have helped restore my confidence, help me buy the right property in the right area. This has given me a passive income to enjoy more of life

Mary T. McKinley

As an added bonus I'd like to share some of the books and resources that I've discussed or promised throughout this book.

Recommended Books or Magazines

Rich Dad Poor Dad - Robert Kiyosaki

Think and Grow Rich - Napoleon Hill

The 80/20 Principle – Richard Kock

The E-Myth – Michael Gerber

Seven Strategies for Wealth & Happiness – Jim Rohn

The 5 Second Rule – Mel Robbins

Take Control of Your Life – Mel Robbins

Goals & Vision Mastery Course – Numerous Authors (Too many to list)

The Best Kept Secrets of Great Communication – Peter Thomson

Success Magazine

Your Property Network Magazine

For the bonuses we promised you earlier in the book to help you on your property journey please go here;

http://bit.ly/PSF-BOOK-BONUSES